CELEBRATING HOLIDAYS

Presidents' Day

by Rachel Grack

BLASTOFF! READERS
2

BELLWETHER MEDIA • MINNEAPOLIS, MN

Note to Librarians, Teachers, and Parents:

Blastoff! Readers are carefully developed by literacy experts and combine standards-based content with developmentally appropriate text.

Level 1 provides the most support through repetition of high-frequency words, light text, predictable sentence patterns, and strong visual support.

Level 2 offers early readers a bit more challenge through varied simple sentences, increased text load, and less repetition of high-frequency words.

Level 3 advances early-fluent readers toward fluency through increased text and concept load, less reliance on visuals, longer sentences, and more literary language.

Level 4 builds reading stamina by providing more text per page, increased use of punctuation, greater variation in sentence patterns, and increasingly challenging vocabulary.

Level 5 encourages children to move from "learning to read" to "reading to learn" by providing even more text, varied writing styles, and less familiar topics.

Whichever book is right for your reader, Blastoff! Readers are the perfect books to build confidence and encourage a love of reading that will last a lifetime!

This edition first published in 2018 by Bellwether Media, Inc.

No part of this publication may be reproduced in whole or in part without written permission of the publisher. For information regarding permission, write to Bellwether Media, Inc., Attention: Permissions Department, 5357 Penn Avenue South, Minneapolis, MN 55419.

Library of Congress Cataloging-in-Publication Data

Names: Koestler-Grack, Rachel A., 1973- author.
Title: Presidents' Day / by Rachel Grack.
Description: Minneapolis, MN : Bellwether Media, Inc., 2018. | Series: Blastoff! Readers: Celebrating Holidays | Includes bibliographical references and index. | Audience: Grades K-3. | Audience: Ages 5-8.
Identifiers: LCCN 2017029518 | ISBN 9781626177543 (hardcover : alk. paper) | ISBN 9781681034591 (ebook)
Subjects: LCSH: Presidents' Day–Juvenile literature.
Classification: LCC E176.8 .K65 2018 | DDC 394.261–dc23
LC record available at https://lccn.loc.gov/2017029518

Editor: Paige V. Polinsky   Designer: Tamara JM Peterson

Printed in the United States of America, North Mankato, MN.

Table of **Contents**

Presidents' Day Is Coming!

Children listen closely to stories about famous United States presidents. They learn what it takes to be a great leader.

White House, Washington, D.C.

It is almost Presidents' Day!

What Is Presidents' Day?

The real name of Presidents' Day is Washington's Birthday. It was meant to honor the first U.S. president, George Washington.

George Washington

The Father of His Country

1775	Washington becomes commander of the American army; Revolutionary War begins.
1781	Washington's troops win the Revolutionary War
1789	Washington becomes the first U.S. president
1792	Washington is reelected as president

Many people celebrate all U.S. presidents on this day.

Who Celebrates Presidents' Day?

Most Americans **observe** Presidents' Day.

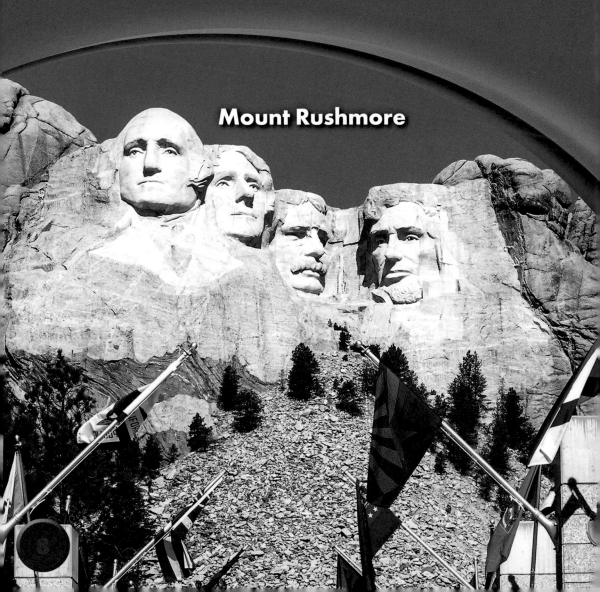

Mount Rushmore

States That Celebrate

official holiday

N
W • E
S

It is not an **official** holiday in some states. But people still celebrate!

George Washington was a brave leader.

Americans wanted to honor him. They began celebrating his birthday, February 22.

Washington's Birthday became
a **federal holiday** in 1879.

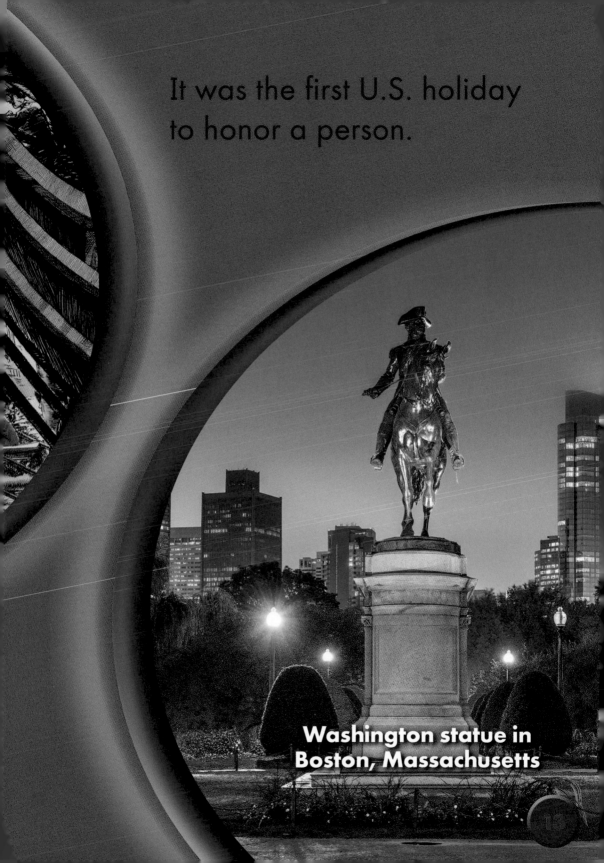

It was the first U.S. holiday to honor a person.

Washington statue in Boston, Massachusetts

In 1971, the holiday moved to the third Monday in February.

Abraham Lincoln

Lincoln Memorial, Washington, D.C.

This falls near **former** president Abraham Lincoln's birthday. Many states renamed it Presidents' Day.

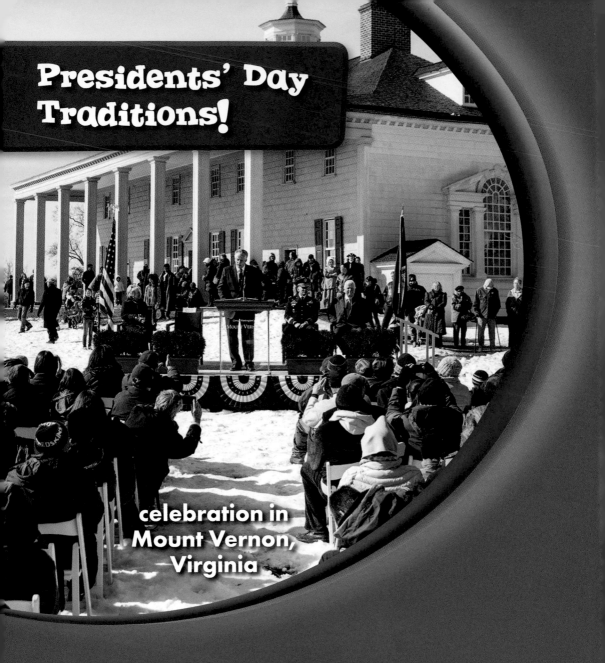

Presidents' Day Traditions!

celebration in
**Mount Vernon,
Virginia**

People celebrate Washington's life.
They remember how he and other
presidents served America.

Make a George Washington Wig

Wear your wig and pretend you are America's first president!

What You Need:
- large paper bag
- marker
- scissors
- glue
- cotton balls
- blue ribbon, 20 inches long

What You Do:

1. Keep the bag folded. Draw a curved line on it as shown.
2. Cut along the line. Be sure to cut through both sides of the bag. Throw away the top part. Open the bottom, and turn it upside down. This is your wig cap.
3. Glue rows of cotton balls to the outside of the cap.
4. Tie the ribbon into a bow. Glue it to the bottom end of the cap to create a ponytail.

17

Some businesses close for the holiday. Many stores offer huge sales.

Children learn about
past presidents.

Some cities hold historical **reenactments.**

Revolutionary War reenactment

George Washington's
Mount Vernon home

Families visit famous historic
places. They take time to honor
the leaders of America!

Glossary

federal holiday—a holiday made law by a country's government; government offices close on federal holidays.

former—earlier

observe—to celebrate

official—publicly known

reenactments—plays that act out events

To Learn More

AT THE LIBRARY

Carr, Aaron. *Presidents' Day*. New York, N.Y.:
Lightbox, 2016.

Dash, Meredith. *Presidents' Day*. Minneapolis,
Minn.: ABDO Kids, 2015.

Gilpin, Caroline Crosson. *George Washington*.
Washington, D.C.: National Geographic, 2014.

ON THE WEB

Learning more about
Presidents' Day is as
easy as 1, 2, 3.

1. Go to www.factsurfer.com.

2. Enter "Presidents' Day" into the search box.

3. Click the "Surf" button and you will see a
   list of related web sites.

With factsurfer.com, finding more information is
just a click away.

Index